The Fairy of Gossamer River

The Fairy of Gossamer River

Zohra Nabi

Felishia Henditirto

Collins

Contents

Chapter 1

Once they left Ms Gillyflower's Finishing School for Fairies, pupils were encouraged to go out into the world and make themselves useful. Fairies were not meant to be lazy, or dull. Ordinary people needed *sparkle*, and that was what fairies were there to give.

The trouble with Yasmina Moonbeam was not that she was lazy, or dull. She had been top of her class in rabbit-taming, and had received high marks in making-boats-from-acorns. Everyone said she would do great things.

And yet here she was, outside Ms Gillyflower's office, without any idea of what she should do now there were no classes to go to.

Ms
Gillyflower

Perhaps I ought to be a teacher, she thought, fluttering her wings anxiously. *Then I would never have to leave school.*

Yasmina did have an unfortunately short temper and could fly into a rage at the drop of a conker, but perhaps teaching would make her more patient.

The office door opened, and Ms Gillyflower's voice floated out.

"Ms Moonbeam?"

Yasmina gulped. Clutching her satchel, she flew into the office and took a seat opposite her head teacher. Ms Gillyflower was a formidable woman – she was close to her 400th birthday, and it was said that she had once been a fairy godmother to a dragon. No one wanted to get on the wrong side of her.

"Now, Ms Moonbeam," the head teacher said, scanning her reports. "You are an *exceptional* pupil."

"Yes, Ms Gillyflower," said Yasmina.

"With an *exceptionally* bright future ahead of you."

"Thank you, Ms Gillyflower."

"And yet you have finished your education here, and still have no good job to go to."

The head teacher sighed, and removed her spectacles, rubbing the bridge of her nose. "A fairy must find out how she can use her talents to make the world a better place. But if you cannot learn to control your anger and work with other people, I worry you never will."

"I could teach here … ?" Yasmina began hopefully. But her teacher waved her away.

"There are no free teaching places. Besides, we all remember the Great Vegetable Disaster last summer."

Yasmina nodded guiltily. She hadn't *meant* to get so cross – but she had accidentally transformed a bullying classmate into a pumpkin, without any idea of how to transform them back. Still, it was unfair of Ms Gillyflower to bring it up. Tessa Willowdean

was *far* less orange than she
had been.

"Now, I may have some
friends who can find you
a job."

Ms Gillyflower snapped
her fingers, and a scroll
appeared out of thin air.
She ran her finger down it.

"*Hmm* – how about this:
there's a princess being
guarded by a dragon
in a tall tower. I'm sure
she would appreciate
a protector with some
kindly advice, and a spell
or two."

Yasmina shifted in her seat. "That sounds great," she said. "It's just … I'm not *fantastic* with dragons. If I get too close to one, I get a bit … wobbly."

Ms Gillyflower sighed. "All right then." She traced her finger down the scroll, which helpfully unfurled itself even more.

"Perhaps we should find you a job in a cottage instead with a thatched roof. You'd be taking care of a small forest. It's hard work, but you would have some local woodland creatures to help you with your chores, and a meadow to gather wildflowers in."

"A meadow? And a thatched roof?" Yasmina replied, her heart sinking. "That sounds lovely, it really does but I have the worst hay fever. I'll never stop sneezing."

"Dear oh dear. You're not making this easy," said Ms Gillyflower. She ran her finger down the scroll again – by this point, it had unfurled so much that it was as long as the neck of a giraffe.

But then Ms Gillyflower paused, her nail coming down triumphantly.

"Aha!" she said. "I have it. A wise woman, who happens to be a dear old friend of mine, is set to retire at the end of the week. She's looking for a hardworking, no-nonsense fairy to replace her, who can help out the local wildlife and look after the environment. I'll send her a message and say I have the perfect person for the job."

"A wise woman?" Yasmina repeated back. "But don't wise women live in cottages too?"

"Not this one," said Ms Gillyflower. "You'll find her at number three, Gossamer River, Little Warbling."

She snapped her fingers, and a neatly-written address card appeared in Yasmina's hands.

"She will see you first thing tomorrow. Now if you don't mind, I'm due at a royal birth ceremony in half an hour. Just remember, whatever job you do, your purpose as a fairy is to make the world *shine*."

She made a shooing motion with her hands, and getting the message, Yasmina flew from the room, only just remembering to say "thank you" as she left.

Ms Gillyflower's vacancies for young fairies

Vacancy 1: Fairy of a tall tower

- Princess in tall tower in need of advice and spells.

- Any applicants must be patient, kind and able to survive dragon fire.

- Warning: Must be good with heights.

Vacancy 2: Fairy Godmother wanted

- Must be able to turn vegetables into vehicles.

- Must have an eye for fashion.

- Must be on time (no missing the midnight deadline!).

Vacancy 3: Tooth Fairy

- Collect teeth from small children and leave a coin behind.
- Warning: Beware of traps left by small children.
- Nervous fairies need not apply.

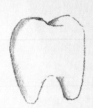

Vacancy 4: Woodland fairy

- Enjoy the forest with woodland creatures!
- Applicants must enjoy gardening, mending and potion-brewing.
- Tumbledown cottage included.

Vacancy 5: Wise woman

- Wise woman wanted for the town of Little Warbling.
- Must enjoy water and wildlife.
- Must be able to face up to wickedness.

Chapter 2

The next morning, Yasmina flew to Gossamer River, clutching her suitcase nervously. What kind of job would she have to do here – and would she be up to it?

As she approached the water, she had to admit it was very beautiful. The river ran crystal clear, with dragonflies and brightly-coloured birds darting to catch insects. There were grassy banks and ferns, and trees surrounding the water, which made the sunlight look green and filled the air with fresh, woody smells. The stream fed into a river just ahead, and lining the river were boats, all of them painted in bright colours, and with names like *Meadowsweet* or *Northstar*.

Suddenly, Yasmina heard a voice.

"You must be Miss Moonbeam?"

Yasmina turned around. The voice had come from one of the long narrow boats – this one was painted a cheerful green with a bright red roof. A black cat was perched on the roof, licking its paws daintily.

"Yes?" said Yasmina, peering down.

A woman emerged from the narrowboat. She was as different from Ms Gillyflower as it was possible to be. Her grey hair was long and curly, her cardigan was a jumble of patchwork, and her wings needed a good polish. Her eyes were very kind.

"Good morning," she said.
"I'm Mrs Fairweather, the wise woman.
I'm delighted that you'll be my replacement –

you look very determined, and that's exactly what you'll need to be."

"Determined?" Yasmina asked, bewildered. But the wise woman appeared not to have heard her.

"Now, your main job will be to open and shut the lock every day," she said, pointing to what looked like a white gate further up the river. "You use the lock to change the level of the water, which allows boats to keep moving smoothly through the waterway.

"Other than that, you should do your best to keep the river clean and look after the wildlife here. If you need any help, you'll find me at the Fenchurch Home for Retired Fairies."

Mrs Fairweather smiled at Yasmina warmly, handed over the manual for working the lock, picked up her cat underneath her arm, and took off into the sky.

Slightly startled by Mrs Fairweather's sudden exit, Yasmina looked around. She had only ever been on school trips to the countryside – where should she begin?

At that moment, a brown, furry creature with a long tail paddled past her and nodded politely. "Good day to you, Madam."

"Argh!" Yasmina screamed. "A rat!"

"A rat?" The creature drew itself up to its full height, looking deeply offended. "Madam, you are mistaking me for one of my common cousins. I am a *water vole* – from a distinguished mammal family. We are *highly* endangered," he added, importantly. "Very rare, you understand."

"Oh," said Yasmina. "I-I'm sorry."

"No harm done," said the water vole, cheerfully. "You'll see me around, I expect – and the family. They're *cultivating* us."

"Cultivating?" asked Yasmina.

"*Mmm.* Encouraging us to settle here. They're very interested in our development." He puffed out his chest. "We have *scientists* coming to visit."

"Don't listen to him," came a voice.

Yasmina turned around. A newt had swum up to the side of the boat and pulled itself out of the water.

"It's *my* family you really want to meet. You might have heard of us – the *great crested newts* you know. We're very famous – the modern dinosaurs, some might say."

"And who are they?" Yasmina said, pointing to a row of four frogs who were all swimming hand in hand. The newt made a hissing noise of disgust.

"Oh. *Them.* They're not proper wildlife at all, you know. I wouldn't bother with them."

"Good morning, fair maiden," the frog who was closest called out, and the row came to a halt in front of the boat. "I don't suppose you are a princess, by any chance?"

"A princess? No – I'm sorry," said Yasmina.

"Ah, no matter," said another of
the frogs, cheerfully. "You see, we were once
princes ourselves – brothers, all of us."

"We lived carefree, happy lives," continued
the second frog, "until a meddling good fairy
decided we needed to learn to 'care about other
people', and 'not be so selfish for a change' and
turned us into frogs."

"She was a rather rude person. But she said we would be frogs until we could prove our unselfishness by having a princess kiss us," said the third frog.

Yasmina frowned. "That doesn't make a lot of sense," she said.

"Well, it was something like that," the fourth frog said, waving his webbed foot airily. "We just swim around, minding our own business and waiting for our princess to come. Don't think too much about what makes *sense*, for your own sake."

"I'll try not to," muttered Yasmina.

25

Yasmina's guide on how to use a lock

How does a boat go uphill? Using a clever invention called a lock. Here's how to use a lock:

1. Open the bottom sluice. Turn the first paddle. This opens the bottom sluice. Water drains downstream (like pulling the plug in a bath).

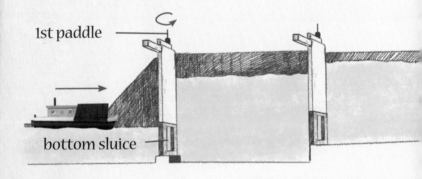

1st paddle

bottom sluice

2. Open the bottom gate. The boat goes through. Close the lower gate and sluice (like putting the plug back in a bath).

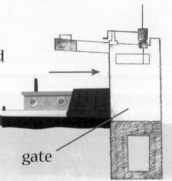

gate

3. Open the top sluice. Turn the second paddle.
Water comes into the lock from upstream
Water level rises, taking the boat up.

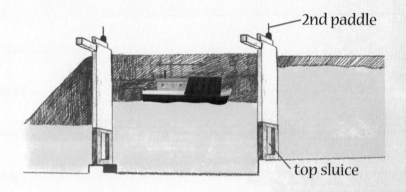

2nd paddle

top sluice

4. When the water inside the lock is level
with the water upstream, open the top
gate to let the boat through.

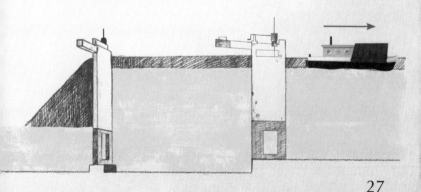

Chapter 3

In spite of her slightly strange introduction to the area, Yasmina soon came to enjoy being the Wise Woman of Gossamer River. Opening the lock was not very difficult, and she enjoyed chatting to the owners of the boats passing through, learning where they had come from and where they were heading off to. Some of them had come right from the opposite end of the country!

It turned out that the river was very long, and it ran through all kinds of places, from big cities to quiet villages in the country. But Yasmina's favourite thing about living on Gossamer River was the wildlife. She was learning something new every day. She learnt that the bright birds she saw were kingfishers, and that grey herons with their long necks lurked among the ferns.

29

Yasmina learnt the difference between a damselfly with its blue-tipped wings and an orange wandering glider. In the evening, she saw pipistrelle bats and scarlet tiger moths swooping low over the water.

In the evenings, she would have a glass of elderflower cordial and write down all the different species she had noticed in her journal, making note of everything she had learnt about them.

But one Wednesday morning, Yasmina awoke to the sound of a large vehicle beeping.

Emerging from her narrow boat, Yasmina rubbed her eyes and stared, barely able to understand what she was seeing.

An enormous lorry was reversing toward the river, coughing out black exhaust fumes and filling the air with the smell of hot rubber. Before she could get over her initial shock, the lorry's doors swung open, and it tipped out a huge load of rubbish into the river.

Yasmina coughed, bringing her hand to her nose as the hot-rubber smell was immediately drowned out by the stink of mouldy bananas, sour milk and rotten potatoes. Meanwhile, filthy water was pouring endlessly into the river from a waste pipe, and Yasmina saw the newts and toads scrambling desperately to the shore to escape it.

The beautiful surroundings of Gossamer River were being treated like a rubbish dump.

"What are you doing?!" Yasmina shrieked at the top of her lungs.

A woman with a blonde ponytail leaned out of the lorry window.

"Hello, love! Just following orders to drop this lorry-load here. If you've got a problem, take it up with the Wizard of Waste."

"*Who*?"

"He runs the big supermarket. This is his rubbish! His office is only ten minutes from here."

Yasmina stormed her way into town. Flying would have been quicker, of course, but she couldn't make her case to the Wizard of Waste without stomping out some of her rage first.

The Wizard of Waste had his office in an enormous glass building, right in the middle of the biggest roundabout in town. It towered above the speeding cars, surrounded by black exhaust fumes and honking horns.

In front of the building were two security guards, who took one look at Yasmina and moved to block her from entering.

Yasmina flicked her wrist, and the doors flung themselves open, as though scared of being told off. Glowering, she stomped past the astonished guards and into the hallway.

Inside, she found rows and rows of shiny offices, with glass walls and doors so that anyone looking in could see how hard the people inside were working.

They were all sitting at identical desks, and their black suits and speedy typing made them seem to Yasmina like particularly superior ants. The only other signs of life were several potted palms, and a receptionist sat underneath a sign which read: *Welcome! How may we help you today?*

Yasmina marched up to him.

"Good morning," she said, remembering her good manners in the nick of time. "I would like to speak with the Wizard of Waste, please."

"The Wizard of Waste is an extremely important man, with extremely important business to attend to," said the receptionist, barely looking up, "but I can arrange an appointment for you for the 31st April? Or the 49th August? Or perhaps the 12th of Never?"

Yasmina ignored him and decided to take matters into her own hands. Flapping her wings, she flew up and up the stairwell, right to the top floor of the very tall tower. She heard the security guards yelling behind her, but she ignored them.

When she reached the top of the stairs, she saw a door in front of her, which read:

**The Office of the Wizard of Waste
CEO of Waste and Want Industries**

*No cleaning staff
are permitted entry.*

With a glower, Yasmina delivered a well-aimed kick right in the middle of the door, and it swung open.

"Ah, Ms Moonbeam," came a rumbling voice from inside. "I understand you wish to see me?"

Yasmina's wildlife observations on Gossamer River

Kingfishers

- Kingfishers catch fish, but they'll also eat tadpoles and water insects if they can get them.
- They have long beaks, and are very good divers.
- Kingfishers nest in tunnels in riverbanks.

Grey herons

- Herons wait patiently in shallow water, with their neck bowed.
- Herons have their nests at the tops of trees.
- They hunt solo but hang out in groups!

Water voles

- Water voles have a complicated maze of tunnels in the banks of the canal – and they don't like leaving their burrows.

- Water voles are very good swimmers.

- They're herbivores, so they enjoy different plants growing alongside Gossamer River, especially grasses and herbs.

Great crested newts

- Male great crested newts have spikes all along their backs – you can tell they're descended from dinosaurs!

- They hibernate during the winter.

- They're nocturnal – you can find them asleep under logs during the day.

Chapter 4

It was difficult to see exactly what the Wizard of Waste looked like, because he was completely surrounded by every kind of rubbish there was. It rose either side of him in piles on his desk. There was a layer of bubble wrap and plastic bags where he had clearly ordered something online and not bothered to return it. There was a layer of fast-food wrappers, with mouldy remains of food still clinging to them.

Finally, there were stacks and stacks of papers. They had become so jumbled that no one could possibly find what they were looking for.

Behind the rubbish, Yasmina could make out a pair of glinting spectacles, and a long white beard with traces of baked beans on it.

"Please," the wizard gestured with his hand. "Take a seat."

Yasmina wrinkled her nose and began to wade through the rubbish.

The only other seat she could see had three empty crisp packets and four apple cores on it.

"Thank you," she said, "but I prefer to stand. Wizard of Waste, I don't suppose you're aware, but today I woke up to find one of your lorries dumping several tonnes of rubbish into Gossamer River!"

"Yes," said the wizard, pleasantly. "Isn't it a good idea?! It seems like the perfect place for a rubbish dump to me."

Yasmina felt herself redden with rage. "What do you mean? It is an utter disgrace – the river smells like bad eggs, the animals are struggling to breathe – no one could possibly swim there or walk along the river now!"

"Precisely! See, this is my plan." The wizard rootled through his pile and came up with a sheet of paper – covered in orange squash stains.

"You see, it's quickest and cheapest for us to dump our waste in the river. But even better, I came to realise that the more disgusting we make the *outside*, the more time people will want to spend *inside* my new shopping centre! Look here."

He hunted through his pile again and pulled out a crumpled plan with chocolate thumbmarks around the edges. The plan had the title – The Wizard of Waste's Wonderful Emporium.

"It will have everything: shops, supermarkets, restaurants. I was even thinking of putting in a petting zoo – and a swimming pool."

"*A petting zoo?*" Yasmina said quietly, forcing herself to count to ten in her head. "You honestly think that could make up for losing the fresh air and wildlife?"

"Yes, I do," said the wizard. "Because when people can no longer see water and wildlife for free, they will be all the more willing to pay for what I can give them in town."

He clapped his hands together. "You seem tense. Why don't you try one of my spa packages? You can request a river soundscape and some forest-scented candles – you'll feel as though you're right in the middle of nature."

"I *am* in the middle of nature!" Yasmina finally exploded, her voice rising to a screech. "I live right slap-bang in the middle of nature, where I can get my forest smells and river sounds for free. A place where the wildlife is wild and doesn't have to sit in cages, waiting for people to gawk at them.

"And I am telling you right now that if you don't stop dumping your disgusting piles of rubbish in our river, I am going to have to stop *you*."

"My goodness!" The wizard smiled at her. "Well, good luck, young lady. Why not give it your best shot, and then in a few weeks' time, when it fails, I'll find you a nice job working in one of my shops."

Yasmina flew as quickly as she could to the Fenchurch Home for Retired Fairies, her wings vibrating with rage. The more she allowed herself to think about what the Wizard of Waste had done, the angrier she grew. But, this time, her anger felt useless. What was the point of losing her temper, if she couldn't change things for the better?

By the time she reached Mrs Fairweather's room and knocked on her door, she was buzzing like a hornet at a children's birthday picnic.

49

Mrs Fairweather opened her door, took one look at Yasmina, and said: "I take it you've had your first meeting with the Wizard of Waste?"

"He's impossible!" Yasmina seethed. "How can he be allowed to get away with it?"

"Because he's rich," said Mrs Fairweather. "Because his businesses make a lot of money for the town. Because he gives some of that money to the right kinds of people, and some of it to the wrong kinds of people. Because people like him will always think they can do whatever they like – and he hates the idea of people enjoying wildlife for free when he could be making money from it. He's unstoppable!"

Wizard of Waste's blueprints for the town centre

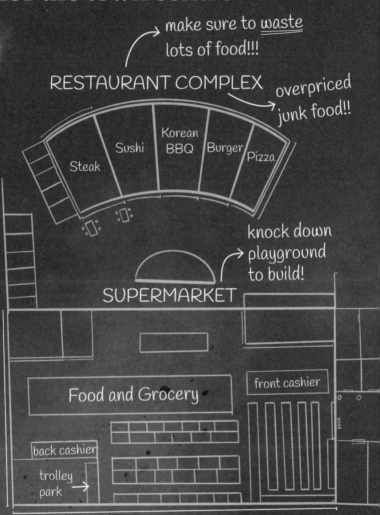

make sure to <u>waste</u> lots of food!!!

RESTAURANT COMPLEX

overpriced junk food!!

Steak Sushi Korean BBQ Burger Pizza

knock down playground to build!

SUPERMARKET

Food and Grocery

front cashier

back cashier

trolley park →

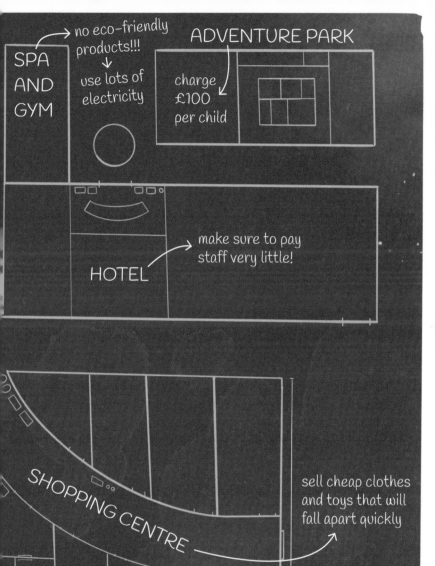

SPA AND GYM

no eco-friendly products!!!

use lots of electricity

ADVENTURE PARK

charge £100 per child

HOTEL

make sure to pay staff very little!

SHOPPING CENTRE

sell cheap clothes and toys that will fall apart quickly

53

Chapter 5

Mrs Fairweather guided Yasmina to a chair and poured out tea for them both.

"I don't understand," Yasmina spluttered. "What's the point of making money for the town if no one can go outside because the air is too polluted, and no one can visit the river because it's filled with rubbish? And never mind the town – what about the frogs and newts and fish – what about the family of water voles? Isn't it *their* town too?"

"I know, I know," Mrs Fairweather sighed. "But what can we do? There's no one powerful enough to put a stop to him. He's been dumping rubbish in rivers for months – it was only a matter of time before he got to Gossamer River."

"What about the people of the town? Surely, they want to protect the river too?" asked Yasmina.

Mrs Fairweather shook her head. "The Wizard of Waste has spent a lot of money on making sure that the people of this town don't get out and enjoy the wildlife – and that includes the river. They don't even remember that Gossamer River exists, most of the time."

Yasmina sipped her tea. Even as she stewed in her rage, an idea was bubbling to the surface of her mind.

"So," she said slowly. "If we could make the townspeople aware of the river, then maybe they would think of it as something they wanted to protect – "

Mrs Fairweather raised an eyebrow. "What do you have in mind?" she asked.

A few days later, there was a small commotion in the town of Little Warbling. A large group clustered around a poster that had been pasted to the door of the supermarket, and even more people were reading newspapers with a large advert in the middle.

"Have you heard?" one man called out to his friend. "There's buried treasure at the bottom of Gossamer River."

"Gold coins and rubies," said someone else. "Diamonds too, I bet. They've announced a reward for the person who finds them!"

Soon, the whole town was abuzz with the news. Even the Mayor of Little Warbling had come out of his office to address the crowd.

"Everyone, meet at Gossamer River!" he said, rubbing his hands together. "We will find this buried treasure together!"

When the whole town of Little Warbling arrived, Yasmina was there waiting for them with a smile. There were even more people than she'd hoped. As they arrived, their expressions of hope turned quickly to horror and disgust at what they saw.

"Good people of Little Warbling," she called out. "I'm afraid we've run into a problem. Look around you! Rubbish and waste have been dumped in *your* river. We'll never find the buried treasure now."

"How could this have happened?" asked one townsperson.

"Who could have done this?" cried another.

The mayor looked embarrassed and mumbled something under his breath.

"We've got to reclaim Gossamer River for the people of this town," she said. "Let's clean up the river, and then we'll be able to see the buried treasure. Who's with me?"

The cheer that went up in the crowd drowned out the mumbling of the mayor.

61

Soon, the whole town was involved in cleaning up the river.

One group were filtering out the food waste with large nets – some were using litter-pickers to pick up plastic bottles and containers.

A group of children had taken on the responsibility of moving the toads and newts to clean, fresh water while the river was being cleaned.

"Make sure to wear gloves, for safety," called out Yasmina. "And children, stay close to a grown-up."

After a few hours, the river was looking cleaner than ever before.

Yasmina could see the riverweeds beneath the water's surface, and the smell of the rubbish was soon replaced with the fresh, muddy scent Yasmina knew and had started to love. Best of all, Yasmina began to hear birdsong again. Amid the green palette of the river, there was the bright blue flash of a kingfisher skimming the water, and the soft grey of a heron hunting on the bank.

"Look at that!" One of the children pointed. "What is it?"

"That's a water vole," said Yasmina, smiling as the creature puffed out his chest. "I'm sure he'd be happy to tell you more about himself."

The children made excited noises. In fact, the more the clean-up went on, the more interested people seemed in the wildlife they were seeing all around them. And the more wildlife they saw, the more they appreciated the cool, clear water around them, and the shade provided by the trees all around. In fact, as the clean-up came to an end, it seemed as though everyone had forgotten there was ever any treasure in the first place.

65

What happens when rivers are polluted?

When plastic is dumped in a river, it will often find its way into the sea.

Plastic increases the risk of animals being poisoned, getting caught or choking.

Sewage in a river can lead to thick algae growing, which makes the river so dark that plants can't grow. If the plants don't grow, animals who need the plants can't live in the river anymore.

Sewage in rivers can lead to high levels of dangerous bacteria, making it unsafe for humans to swim there.

Chapter 6

Yasmina stood on the roof of her narrow boat and addressed the crowd again.

"Thank you so much to everyone for coming out. I'm delighted to say that the river is now crystal clear and shining. Unfortunately, there does not appear to be any buried treasure.

"But *listen*. Gossamer River is free for you to use and enjoy. You can spot wildlife; you can sit on the banks and dip your toes in the water; you can walk here with your families and enjoy the beautiful views. Isn't that something worth protecting? Isn't that something we should all *treasure*?"

She turned meaningfully to the mayor, who cleared his throat.

"Ms Moonbeam is right. From now on, dumping waste in the river is *strictly* forbidden. What's more, the town will fund fortnightly river activities for children, led by yourself, Ms Moonbeam – if you would like."

Yasmina felt her chest flutter with happiness. She had only hoped that people would know they could enjoy the river – she hadn't imagined that they might want to learn to take care of it, too.

Everything seemed too good to be true. Until she heard a familiar, unpleasant voice coming from far too close behind her.

"And what is the meaning of all this?" asked the Wizard of Waste.

Yasmina, now perfectly calm herself, turned around.

"Isn't it wonderful?!" she told the wizard. "The whole town got together to clean up the river. And the mayor has announced that no one will be allowed to fill it with rubbish ever again."

The smile slid off the Wizard of Waste's face. "And what is the meaning of this?" he asked the mayor. "What about all the money I gave to your office last Monday?"

The mayor looked sheepish.

"Your DONATION was very much appreciated," the mayor said loudly, in case any of the townspeople were listening. "But the people of this town wish to enjoy the river – and at the end of the day, I work for *them*."

The Wizard of Waste was scowling now. He turned to the townspeople. "Surely you don't want to be here – it's filthy, and full of frogs and creepie-crawlies. Surely, you'd rather be at the new swimming pool I'm building?"

"That's not a frog," a small child informed the wizard. "That's a great crested newt. Did you know they're descended from dinosaurs?"

The wizard's scowl deepened. He turned on Yasmina, who stood her ground. As the wizard advanced at her angrily, he didn't notice the four frogs creeping up behind him.

"You may have won back your little stretch of river," he spat. "But I will win. People don't want nature, not really. They want things they can buy – things that they can spend their money on. And so long as that's the case, they'll always come crawling back to me-*eeeee*!"

The Wizard of Waste broke off with a howl as his arms and legs were grabbed by four frogs, and he was dragged into the river. There, armed with eco-friendly soap and flannels, they proceeded to clean him *extremely* thoroughly.

"No!" the wizard shouted. "Not soap! Anything but soap! I'm a Wizard of Waste – all my power comes from dirt!"

But the frogs didn't listen. After a few minutes, the wizard slunk out from the river and back towards the town, so clean that his white beard was gleaming. He looked very sorry for himself.

To Yasmina's surprise, she was suddenly surrounded by four young men, all in capes and gold crowns, picking pondweed out of their hair.

"Goodness me," said one of the princes, in a croaking voice, "I suppose that must have done it. We're humans again."

"B-but I thought you had to be kissed by a princess?" asked Yasmina.

The princes shrugged their shoulders.

"Did we really say that?" asked one. "You know, I think we might have misremembered.

"In fact," added another, "I think I might have made up the whole princess-kiss thing. The good fairy only mentioned us becoming unselfish."

"Indeed, I did," came a voice.

Yasmina jumped at the sound. Standing behind her was Ms Gillyflower, who was looking at the scene with a distinctly proud air.

77

"Well, Ms Moonbeam. I think you've done yourself and my school credit. You've used your determination to improve your environment, you kept your temper with the Wizard of Waste, and you worked with other people to make the world a better place. How did you manage to make such a success of your first job?"

Yasmina grinned and looked around at the river. The water was so clear now that the sunbeams were bouncing off the surface, catching the light like tiny splinters of glass.

"Well, Ms Gillyflower, I followed your advice," said Yasmina. "I tried to make the world *shine*."

Canals and rivers

Rivers are naturally-formed meandering waterways that usually flow into the sea or lakes.

Canals are long stretches of waterways dug by humans – a bit like water roads!

More about canals

- Canals were used a lot in Victorian times for transporting materials all over the UK.

- The kind of habitats provided by canals include grassland, scrubland (areas with low trees and bushes) and banks where wildflowers can grow.

- Old buildings along canals such as bridges and tunnels make great safe habitats for wildlife.

- Because of the range of habitats, canals can support a variety of wildlife, both animals and plants.

- The Canal & River Trust says there are over 3,000 kilometres of connected habitats made possible by canals. The hedgerows, trees and grassland provide a "superhighway" for insects and animals!

Yasmina's conservation tips

Hello! The Mayor of Little Warbling has asked me to lead river conservation classes. Conservation means taking care of something, so I thought I'd give a little guide.

1. Go for a walk by your nearest river or canal and note the different plants and animals you see. The more we know about our rivers and canals, the better!

2. Cut down on single-use plastics – they can end up in animal habitats. Try using a reuseable water bottle and remember your "bag for life" when you go to the shops!

3. Look at competitions run by the Canal & River Trust – there are always new ways to get involved in conserving our waterways.

4. Consider joining volunteer campaigns to go litter-picking along rivers. Don't try and litter-pick by yourself – your safety is the most important thing!

5. Finally, remember the main responsibility is on the people in charge. If you're worried about the rivers in your area, write a letter or email to your MP! They should be able to tell you what they're doing to protect local environments.

Sunday, 23 April 2023

FIERCE FAIRY
SAVES OUR RIVER

Warbler

Thanks to the efforts of Yasmina Moonbeam, Gossamer River has been saved from becoming a rubbish dump.

Ms Moonbeam led the townsfolk in cleaning up the river. The mayor's office have also said that the water will be treated to remove harmful chemicals and bacteria. As a result, the water will officially be safe enough for both people and wildlife to enjoy.

Meanwhile, the Wizard of Waste was caught trying to flee Little Warbling late last night. Carrying suitcases of money.

Speaking to *The Little Warbler*, Ms Moonbeam said: "These rivers and streams belong to everyone. We have a duty to protect them as much as we can."

About the author

Why did you want to be an author?

I love writing, specifically creating worlds and characters. Now I can do that all day, rather than having to write in between classes.
Being an author is my dream career!

Zohra Nabi

What is it like for you to write?

It depends. On a day when the stars align and I know how I want the story to unfold, it's the most amazing feeling in the world. I start with a rough outline, but I love the feeling of the story flowing like water, taking you in a different direction than you previously imagined. On days where I'm less sure about where I want it to go, it's like dragging a ton of bricks but sometimes those days can be the most satisfying!

Why this book?

The quality of our water has been in the news a lot recently, and a story involving river pollution has definitely been playing on my mind. I wanted to write a heroine fierce enough to take on the forces destroying our wildlife.

What do you hope readers will get out of the book?

I hope readers will have a sense of how precious our rivers and streams are and maybe that they'll be encouraged to explore and protect their local river!

What sort of fairy would you like to be?

I think I'd like the woodland fairy job. Unlike Yasmina I don't have hayfever, and so getting a tumbledown cottage with a meadow full of wildflowers sounds ideal!

Is Gossamer River based on a real place?

It is! Last year I was studying in Oxford, and on one side of my flat was a gorgeous stretch of water called Castle Mill Stream! I saw so much amazing wildlife, and walking up the towpath used to lift my mood after a long day of lectures.

What's your favourite natural place to visit?

Richmond Park, which has lovely trees, and a botanical garden, and herds of deer. During lockdown it was amazing to have a connection to the natural world nearby.

Do you do things to help wildlife where you live?

I do, I sign petitions and talk to my MP! And I try to support local initiatives. I'm lucky to live in an area where everyone is very committed to conservation and preserving our natural habitat.

About the illustrator

I'm Felishia, a 23-year-old illustrator from Indonesia. I was born in Bandung and raised in a small city called Sumedang. Growing up in a mechanic shop with broken spare parts, and leaking oil always made my childhood filled with adventure. I'm an adventure-seeker, always looking forward for the next adventure.

Felishia Henditirto

What made you want to be an illustrator?

Stories! My mum used to take me to a big bookstore in the city, I would then spent the next 24 hours reading everything I bought, even staying up all night or in school! With illustration I feel like I have a magic wand to tell "stories". In my opinion, illustration is like a powerful language to communicate.

What did you like best about illustrating this book?

Planning the layout! I love thinking about what angle will look fun, where the light and shadow is and how to make the transition from the illustrations to the text. (Also, I unexpectedly enjoy making frogs!)

Is there anything in this book that relates to your own experiences?

Yes, I relate so much to the first chapter when Yasmina isn't sure about what she will do in the future!

How do you bring a character to life in an illustration?

I usually start with imagining their life, their personalities, how they will react to something. I also imagine their hobbies, likes or dislikes and even their backgrounds.

What sort of fairy would you like to be?

I think I would love to be an explorer fairy!

Exploring the unexpected wonder of nature, finding a lost treasure or recording a new species.

Which character was the most fun to draw? Why?

The four princes (in their frog form!). I love how they look expressive despite the super-simple design.

Do you generally prefer drawing goodies or baddies? Why?

Baddies! I think it's because I am a goodie in real life so baddies seem exciting and different.

Is there a spot in nature that inspires your art?

I love the woods! It feels magical and like there could be something coming from inside it. (But I also like the sea and mountains, so I think I like everything in nature.)

Book chat

Which character
did you like best,
and why?

Did your mood
change while you were
reading the book?
If so, how?

If you could
change one thing
about this book,
what would it be?

If you had
to give the book a
new title, what
would you choose?

Which part of
the book did
you like best,
and why?

Have you ever
seen any of the
animals mentioned
in the book?

What sort of fairy
would you like to be?
Why?

Do you think Yasmina
changed between
the start of the story
and the end? If so, how?

Book challenge: Write your top three
tips for conservation.

Collins
BIG CAT

Published by Collins
An imprint of HarperCollins*Publishers*

The News Building
1 London Bridge Street
London SE1 9GF
UK

Macken House
39/40 Mayor Street Upper
Dublin 1
D01 C9W8
Ireland

ISBN 978-0-00-862480-4

British Library Cataloguing-in-Publication Data
A catalogue record for this publication is available
from the British Library.

Download the teaching notes and
word cards to accompany this book at:
http://littlewandle.org.uk/signupfluency/

Get the latest Collins Big Cat news at
collins.co.uk/collinsbigcat

Author: Zohra Nabi
Illustrator: Felishia Henditirto (Astound Illustration
    Agency)
Publisher: Lizzie Catford
Product manager: Caroline Green
Series editor: Charlotte Raby
Commissioning editor: Suzannah Ditchburn
Development editor: Catherine Baker
Project manager: Emily Hooton
Content editor: Daniela Mora Chavarría
Copyeditor: Catherine Dakin
Proofreader: Gaynor Spry
Cover designer: Sarah Finan
Typesetter: 2Hoots Publishing Services Ltd
Production controller: Katharine Willard

Collins would like to thank the teachers and
children at the following schools who took part in
the trialling of Big Cat for Little Wandle Fluency:
Burley And Woodhead Church of England Primary
School; Chesterton Primary School; Lady Margaret
Primary School; Little Sutton Primary School;
Parsloes Primary School.

MIX
Paper | Supporting
responsible forestry
FSC
www.fsc.org
FSC™ C007454